CRIES FOR A L

CRIES FOR A LOST HOMELAND

Reflections on Jesus' Words from the Cross

Guli Francis-Dehqani

CANTERBURY
PRESS
Norwich

© Guli Francis-Dehqani 2021

First published in 2021 by the Canterbury Press Norwich
Editorial office
3rd Floor, Invicta House
108–114 Golden Lane
London EC1Y 0TG, UK
www.canterburypress.co.uk

Canterbury Press is an imprint of
Hymns Ancient & Modern Ltd (a registered charity)

Hymns Ancient & Modern® is a registered trademark of
Hymns Ancient & Modern Ltd
13A Hellesdon Park Road, Norwich,
Norfolk NR6 5DR, UK

All rights reserved. No part of this publication may be reproduced,
stored in a retrieval system, or transmitted,
in any form or by any means, electronic, mechanical,
photocopying or otherwise, without the prior permission of
the publisher, Canterbury Press.

The Author has asserted her right under the Copyright, Designs and
Patents Act 1988 to be identified as the Author of this Work

Scripture quotations are from New Revised Standard Version Bible:
Anglicized Edition, copyright © 1989, 1995 National Council of
the Churches of Christ in the United States of America. Used by
permission. All rights reserved worldwide.

'The Diamond Takes Shape' and 'A Great Need' are from the
Penguin publication *The Gift: Poems by Hafiz*, by Daniel Ladinsky
copyright 1999 and used with permission.

British Library Cataloguing in Publication data

A catalogue record for this book is available
from the British Library

ISBN 978-1-78622-383-8

Printed and bound in Great Britain by
CPI Group (UK) Ltd

Contents

*Dedicated to the faithful remnant
of the Church in Iran*

The diamond takes shape slowly
With integrity's great force,
And from
The profound courage to never relinquish love.

Hafiz, version by David Ladinsky[1]

Foreword

BY SAMUEL WELLS

'Who *are* you?' It's a question habitually asked two-thirds of the way through the film, when the spouse of the time-traveller finally wakes up to the fact that hither-to unexplained absences are all due to their being in a different century for long periods at a time. It's a question Pontius Pilate understandably asks Jesus when he realises that what he's dealing with is no ordinary rabble-rousing Palestinian peasant. It's a question the disciples are entitled to ask when Jesus calms a storm without breaking sweat. It's a question that occupies many people's thoughts about themselves today, as identity becomes the focus of so much searching, controversy and dispute, particularly when old binaries and tired stereotypes are being moved aside.

It's a question one might ask of Guli Francis-Dehqani. Yes, we know, she is the Bishop of Chelmsford. There was a time when that would have been all one needed to know – because to be in such a role would have meant a person had been to a certain kind of school and a particular kind of university and doubtless have come from a family whose course in life had traversed a very limited number of professions or social locations. Today, mercifully, one can no longer assume any of those things; but one can still expect that this is a person the Church considers worthy of people's trust, and – not to raise the stakes too high – full of the Holy Spirit.

But she's also a person from what's clumsily known as a minority ethnic background. She's spent a lot of her life outside England, where it turns out that the ways of the Church of England are not universally admired or imitated, and where the issues are not identical to those that furrow the Anglican brow, and tend to be more pressing and more significant. She knows what it means to be in a minority and sometimes in danger because of her faith. And yet she has also spent a lot of her life in England, and has had to learn how self-absorbed this country and its established Church can be. And here she's discovered something different: what it means to be in a minority and sometimes in danger because of her race. When she speaks of the poignancy of the word 'paradise' in Jesus' phrase, 'Today you will be with me in paradise', she speaks as a Persian woman spotting a Persian word – 'paradise'.

But are these things at the heart of who Guli Francis-Dehqani is? Is not the defining experience of her life the terrifying and devastating upheaval of the Islamic Revolution of 1979, and the kidnapping and murder of her beloved brother? She is a survivor of extreme danger and hovering oppression. When it comes to lived experience of circumstances not unlike those in which Jesus was arrested and executed, she's near the front of the queue. Would not such a life event transform, damage or at least shape the rest of one's life – such that, when asked, 'Who are you?' one might reply, 'I am a traumatised and bereaved refugee.'

So many identities. But when you meet Guli Francis-Dehqani, you realise she has not chosen to let any of these dramatic – even exotic – veils define who she is. She knows *whose* she is, so she has no problem knowing *who* she is. She is a baptised member of the body of Christ. The rest is incidental detail – fascinating, rich, absorbing, about which she talks intriguingly and humbly, without dissemblance or exaggeration, always with tenderness and grace – but not, ever, the central point in question. Her story is the stuff of autobiographies, of grief hidden by darkened glasses, of chapters unspoken because they are too painful, of attempts to deflect into ministry the questions unresolved about identity. But that's not what she believes her story to be. Her story is the one found in these pages – of the realisation that this person, fully a human person and fully a person of the Holy Trinity, his story, his love for the loveless, that they may lovely be, has become her story. Here might she stand and sing – 'No story so divine'.

And sing she does. These pages are her song. Here you will find Christ's story inscribed on her own flesh, and her story inhabited by Christ's flesh. Here you will see her questioning mind and humble heart and searching soul. Here, though you might be meeting Guli for the first time, you will meet Christ as if for the first time, and will want to spend more time with both of them. For the key to understanding Guli is that you can't tell her story without retelling Christ's story.

I once knew a married couple who had come to believe that they were so close that they were, in their words, 'practically indistinguishable'. I've never been sure that was so desirable. But these pages show you something much more admirable. They show you what it means to take up your cross and walk close to Christ. There is no social distancing in Guli's walk with Jesus. And by the time that walk is done, we can't yet be sure what Jesus looks like. But we know who Guli looks like.

Which is why, by the time you finish this book, you will want to look like her.

The Revd Dr Samuel Wells
St Martin-in-the-Fields

Introduction

It was only in my adulthood that I began to realise not only how unusual my childhood had been but what a profound impact it had had – and continues to have – on shaping who I've become. I suspect that's true for most of us. The present is very much woven out of the past and together these give character to the future. In the words of the Irish author John Connolly: 'in every adult dwells the child that was, and in every child waits the adult that will be.'[2]

This realisation of the significance of my childhood developed for me during my early thirties, when I was working towards a doctorate. A series of unexpected twists in my life led me to do the research, and the area I settled on was a study of women missionaries in Iran in the late nineteenth and early twentieth centuries.[3] The topic covered various interests I had, including church history, interfaith studies and feminist theology. As well as being Iranian myself, I was also a product of the efforts of missionaries, and I thought the personal angle would give me an added focus, keep me engaged in the topic over the years it would take to complete the PhD. In the event, a whole new vista opened up for me. The more I learned and the deeper I went, the greater I felt the tug of my roots and the desire to understand myself more completely.

Having left Iran some 15 years earlier, and still unable to return, I began to feel closer and closer to my country of origin and the Church that had nurtured my early faith, even as the physical gulf between us seemed, impossibly, to expand. The longing to go back would sometimes manifest itself, quite literally, as a physical ache in the chest and so, unable as I was to satisfy the yearning, I simply delved deeper into trying to understand the complexity of my past – to make peace with it, to learn from it; in short, to discover who I really was. I learned too that 'the home you leave behind, the one you grew up in, travels ahead and is always there in some form to greet you.'[4] And that learning has continued over many years as I've tried to make sense of the various threads of my life and so be reconciled to who I am. In the words of Farifteh Robb, like me an Iranian Christian in Britain: 'It is this reconciliation that has bestowed upon me the unexpected gift of abundant grace.'[5]

The youngest of four children, I was born and grew up in Iran, in the beautiful city of Isfahan. I was given the name Gulnar, which means 'pomegranate flower', but was always known as Guli – 'little flower' – for short. My father, Hassan, was a Muslim convert from a small village in the centre of the country, and my mother, Margaret, the daughter and granddaughter of missionaries, herself born and raised in Iran. We were part of the tiny Anglican Church that came into being as a result of missionary endeavours in the nineteenth century. The Diocese of Iran was created in 1912, and in 1961 my father became the first indigenous Persian bishop. In 1976 the diocese became part of the newly formed Province of Jerusalem and the Middle East, with my father as the first Presiding Bishop. I grew up bilingually, with Christian influences at home, and the world of Islam at school and in wider society.

This rather unusual childhood was what I considered normal. It was all I knew and, for the most part, my two worlds of school and wider society on the one hand, and home and church life on the other, coexisted reasonably peaceably with some occasional overlap. As the Islamic Revolution of 1979 swept across the country, life changed dramatically. Properties and Christian institutions – such as hospitals and schools – were confiscated or closed down, offices and the Bishop's House were raided, and one of the clergy, the Revd Arastoo Sayyah, was found murdered in his study. More widely, the whole country descended into chaos; curfew was introduced, schools were closed and there were daily demonstrations on the streets. My father was briefly imprisoned before surviving an attack on his life in which my mother was injured. Several months later, while my father was out of the country for meetings, my brother, Bahram, who was 24 and teaching at the University in Tehran, was murdered. No one was ever brought to justice but the family have always understood that he was a scapegoat for our father, who was then advised by friends and colleagues that it was unsafe to return. After Bahram's funeral we joined my father in England, expecting to be home within a few months.[6]

That was not to be and, having arrived in the UK as a refugee aged 14, here I still am, over 40 years later, and now a fully fledged British citizen. My father continued working as Bishop in Iran in exile until his retirement, and dedicated his life to supporting and encouraging Christians still in Iran, working with Persians in this country and writing and translating Christian literature in Persian. Both my parents have now died.

So that's the background and context for this small book, which began life as a series of Good Friday talks. In these reflections I've told my story in greater depth and through the lens of Jesus' last words from the cross. It's been cathartic. But there's another reason for this book too. We tell our stories to connect better with others – to understand ourselves, yes, but also to open channels of communication and understand one another better, developing empathy and compassion. Storytelling has a sacred quality about it: 'It is a way to mine deep down and touch the tender heart of the most defensive adversary'.[7] I hope that some of the themes in this book will resonate with others and help them make sense of their stories. For the most part, the themes are universal – an exploration of our shared humanity and the place of faith within it. So, borrowing words from Annette Simmons, 'My hope is that by talking about my stories, you will start thinking about your own stories'; and it's worth remembering that 'your soul tells the most moving story of all. Go tell your story; the world needs it.'[8]

The inside front cover of this book shows a tile that sits above the entrance to St Luke's Church, Isfahan, and the inside back cover shows it in situ. Using the art of calligraphy so beloved of Iranians, in the centre are the words 'Jesus Christ', and all around are eight descriptions of his character and being: founder; advocate; intermediary; servant; weight bearer; lover; sacrifice; guide. These descriptions find their place in the folds of the narrative that follows, sometimes explicitly, more often implicitly. They are flesh for the bones and help me find meaning in my story. But they also open windows on to the vast mystery that is God. They remind me that so much remains unknown and unknowable. These words breathe life into those things that cannot be fully explained or understood. They appear individually on the opening pages of the sections of the book.

So the book connects me with my past – through memory and imagination, through the poetry of Hafiz and in Persian patterns and illustrations, all reminders of a lost homeland. But the book is also an expression of my desire to connect with others – to know my place of belonging and, through the expansive window of faith, to meet with others in their places of belonging. Writing the reflections helped me articulate my sense of hope for the future despite the pain – and I hope in some small way it might help others to do the same.

Guli Francis-Dehqani
Spring 2021

Acknowledgements

This book would not have come into being without the support, encouragement and friendship of many. I cannot possibly name them all but I do want to express particular thanks to the following. By inviting me to deliver the 2019 Good Friday talks in St Martin-in-the-Fields, the Revd Dr Samuel Wells set the ball rolling and provided the opportunity for me to commit to paper thoughts that had been rattling around for years. Like many others, I continue to be fed and inspired by Sam's own writings, and I'm especially grateful that he agreed to provide the Foreword for this book, which is both profound and humbling. During Holy Week 2021, I was invited by the Very Revd David Monteith, Dean of Leicester, to record abridged and slightly amended versions of these reflections to form online Holy Week meditations in lockdown. David has become a dear friend during my three years in Leicester Diocese, and I've valued his gentle wisdom and humour. I'm so pleased he's contributed to this book in the form of an Afterword from Holy Saturday. In the months leading up to publication I had the good fortune to meet Pádraig Ó Tuama and was absolutely delighted when he agreed to contribute his hitherto unpublished poem 'The Tree of Knowledge' to this book (it is reproduced just before David's Afterword). I'm not a poet – I wish I were – but for me faith is more poetry than prose, and so I'm grateful to Pádraig for enriching this volume. My thanks also go to the Revd Canon Mark Oakley for his advice, and to Christine Smith and all at Canterbury Press.

Had they still been alive, I know my parents would have been delighted by this book. They provided me with the greatest gifts of all, which were to sow the seeds of faith and give me the security that comes from being loved. A day doesn't go by without my thinking of them. They were an extraordinary couple who touched the lives of many and continue still to have a profound influence on my life. And finally, thanks are due to my husband Lee and our three children, Gabriel Iraj, Eleanor Nargess and Simeon Omid. Lee has been by my side for well over half my life now, and his love, friendship and loyal support have been constant throughout. By coming into our lives the children released something within me and freed me to become the person I now am. They are precious beyond words. I live in the hope that one day Lee and the children will visit Iran, see the place where I grew up and experience the country that continues to beckon me home.

I

'Father, forgive'

I

'Father, forgive'

When they came to the place that is called The Skull, they crucified Jesus there with the criminals, one on his right and one on his left. Then Jesus said, 'Father, forgive them; for they do not know what they are doing.' And they cast lots to divide his clothing. And the people stood by, watching; but the leaders scoffed at him, saying, 'He saved others; let him save himself if he is the Messiah of God, his chosen one!' The soldiers also mocked him, coming up and offering him sour wine, and saying, 'If you are the King of the Jews, save yourself!' There was also an inscription over him, 'This is the King of the Jews.'

Luke 23.33–38

Forgiveness – such a well-known concept (for good or ill), and this is where it begins, or at least where its power is located and its challenge to us is focused: at the cross of Jesus. Jesus, at his most helpless and at the point of greatest suffering, uttering the cry of forgiveness for his persecutors and, in so doing, setting the bar for us to do the same – to adopt a posture of forgiveness towards those who do us harm, who hurt us, whose words and actions cause us pain and anguish.

Luke's is the only Gospel in which this, the first of Jesus' seven last words from the cross, is recorded. During these few verses Luke digresses from the familiar account and goes his own way. But more than that, it may surprise some of you that the words 'Father, forgive them; for they do not know what they are doing' do not in fact appear in all the ancient manuscripts. They're missing from some versions of Luke's Gospel. The general view is that Luke must have intended for the words to be included – apart from anything else, they mirror so perfectly his account of the martyrdom of Stephen recorded in Acts chapter 7, where he too utters a similar cry at the point of death by stoning. It's possible that the words were omitted in certain Gospel manuscripts because of the belief among some Christians that the crucifixion of Jesus was of a different order – beyond the pale; an unforgivable sin.

In any case, though it seems likely that the words are authentic, this confusion seems to me to reflect something of our anomalous and difficult relationship with the doctrine of forgiveness. Some recoil from the whole idea; others find it too painful and just impossible; some use it to accuse Christians of being spineless and soft on crime and wrongdoing; still others have embraced it and tried to make it a way of life.

Whatever you think of it, forgiveness is a central Christian theme that we can't simply ignore. We must grapple with it and try to make sense of it. It has, undoubtedly, been misused and exploited down the centuries. It has been oversimplified, misunderstood and perhaps even abused by the Church, which has sometimes sought to force it on people in a controlling, manipulative way, leading individuals to remain in abusive relationships and to suffer ongoing horrors in silence. That is *not* how I understand forgiveness. It is not about tolerating injustice for the sake of it, or acquiescing in harm that belittles human life and dignity. Embracing forgiveness doesn't mean giving up on justice or working for change. The church community in Iran, for example, where my early faith was nurtured and which has suffered so much persecution over the past 40 years, has sought to model the way of forgiveness while not giving up its cry for justice and for the rule of law. In the immediate aftermath of the Revolution, even as my father – who was a Muslim convert and Anglican Bishop in Iran – faced threats of arrest and violence, he never desisted from speaking out against the injustices the Church was undergoing. He wrote letters to the highest authorities, sought support from within and without the country, and made known to any who would listen the iniquities being perpetrated in the name of Islam.

So having tried to establish what forgiveness is *not*, I'd like now to share a few reflections on how I understand forgiveness, offering some windows through which we may contemplate this most testing of Christian ideas.

It strikes me as interesting that this is Jesus' first saying, uttered early in the process of his cruel crucifixion, perhaps before the depths of agony and torment have truly kicked in. He voices his intention, his desire for the reality of forgiveness to be manifest, before he's at a stage at which he might no longer have the strength to do so. Forgiveness is less a point of arrival at some clearly defined destination and more of a messy voyage – the ultimate expedition – undertaken in faith, knowing that we may stumble, fall and fail over and over again. But the yearning to be forgiving is, in itself, a remarkable beginning.

I met an elderly lady recently called Margaret, who told me that her grandson was in prison. I asked if she was able to visit and she said she hadn't been, because she couldn't yet forgive him. I asked if she wanted to, and she said: 'Yes, I do, and one day maybe I'll be able to.' Margaret has unknowingly started on the journey that, unsurprisingly, she couldn't articulate in all its complexity, overlaid as it was with emotions of betrayal, anger, embarrassment and hurt. There may be many twists and turns and complications ahead, but she has opened the door and is leaning into a future with possibilities, rather than one where there are only dead ends.

As the Islamic Revolution in Iran was beginning to take hold – in the early days, as its impact was gradually being felt by the Anglican Church through various raids on properties and confiscation of institutions, as missionaries and foreigners began to depart, leaving the community exposed and vulnerable – I remember a sermon preached by my father. I must have been only around 12 years old but it clearly made an impact on me and I still recall it well. Aware that even greater dangers probably lay ahead, for himself and for his tiny flock, he declared his intention to side with forgiveness rather than hatred. He talked of having preached for years about the theory of forgiveness, but that now it was time to practise it.

He didn't know then that soon he would be in prison, his wife would be injured in an attack on their lives, and that eventually his only son would be murdered and he and his family forced into exile, where he would remain until his death in 2008. But he declared his intention early on to live with a spirit of forgiveness no matter what and, though this proved far from easy, that is the path he and

6

my mother continued to travel and which I have tried to emulate.

Forgiveness is truly not the easy option; it is costly, messy and painful but it does open up the way of *life*. It prevents us getting stuck in the past, held fast in the grip of hatred and bitterness, and it allows also for the possibility of change in the one who has offended. It is a recognition that nothing and no one is beyond redemption; that the way things *have* been isn't the way things need be in future; that good can come out of evil; that love can overwhelm hatred.

Now those who are offered forgiveness, to fully experience it, must choose to embrace it in a spirit of remorse and repentance – but the offer of it is the beginning, and that offer is the scandal of Christianity, for it is open to all, no matter who you are or what you have done. And it is a reminder too that we are, none of us, perfect and that we are on this journey together. All of us need forgiveness in our own lives, for our shortcomings and failures, our sins great and small.

In all this talk of being forgiving, it's worth remembering that forgiveness isn't always *our* gift to offer. Sometimes the greatest offence hasn't been committed against us or at least not only us. When my brother, Bahram, was murdered, it was *his* life that had been cut short. The loss caused us terrible pain, but was it our role to forgive his murderers? Did we even have the right to do this on his behalf? Moreover, is forgiveness ever ours to offer, or does it belong to God? Neither St Stephen as he was being stoned, nor Jesus from the cross, said: 'I forgive.' Their cry is '*Father*, forgive them; for they do not know what they are doing.'

And in the phrase 'for they do not know what they are doing', I don't think there is a suggestion that the offenders get off scot-free – that they shouldn't take responsibility for their actions. Rather, in this act of evil, their *very humanity has been diminished*, and so only God can forgive. This is a significant distinction. Margaret, whose grandson is in prison, is struggling to do the forgiving when perhaps her eyes are set on a target she doesn't need to aim towards. To ask God to forgive is to trust God and surrender to God's will the task of judging and of changing hearts and minds. It is to release us from the burden of responsibility and liberate us to move into the future.

Which brings me to the heart of what forgiveness is – the starting place for hope. Even as I was grieving for the loss of my brother, coping with the rupture from friends and home, stranded in a new and unfamiliar place, I saw my parents travel the painful path towards embracing forgiveness for those who murdered their son. Through my teens, I watched them adjust with graciousness to life in exile and the apparent disintegration of all they had worked for in Iran. And as I watched, I began to realise that what they were doing was *continuing to hope* when all seemed lost.

I cannot end my reflections on forgiveness, and how it ties in with hope, without sharing the prayer my father wrote after my brother was killed. It was read, in the original Persian, at Bahram's funeral in Isfahan. This is the English translation, which has become known as the forgiveness prayer.[9]

O God, *we remember not only Bahram but his
murderers.*

*Not because they killed him in the prime of his youth
and made our hearts bleed and our tears flow.*

*Not because with this savage act they have brought
further disgrace on the name of our country among
the civilised nations of the world.*

*But because through their crime we now follow more
closely your footsteps in the way of sacrifice.*

*The terrible fire of this calamity burns up all selfishness
and possessiveness in us.*

*Its flame reveals the depth of depravity, meanness and
suspicion, the dimension of hatred and the measure
of sinfulness in human nature.*

*It makes obvious as never before our need to trust
in your love as shown in the cross of Jesus and his
resurrection:*

*Love which makes us free from all hatred towards our
persecutors;*

*Love which brings patience, forbearance, courage,
loyalty, humility, generosity and greatness of heart;*

*Love which more than ever deepens our trust in God's
final victory and his eternal designs for the Church
and for the world;*

*Love which teaches us how to prepare ourselves to face
our own day of death.*

O God,

*Bahram's blood has multiplied the fruit of the Spirit
in the soil of our souls: so when his murderers stand
before you on the Day of Judgment, remember the fruit
of the Spirit by which they have enriched our lives, and
forgive.*

Latterly it has struck me forcibly that although the word 'hope' is never used, this prayer is infused with the idea of hope. It defines forgiveness as the thing that enables us to trust more completely. Forgiveness frees us from hatred, allows us to love and releases us from the anxiety of our own death. I wish now that I had quizzed my father about it more while he was still alive, but it seems to me that the prayer is brimming with hope-filled sentiments. What he seemed to be saying was that you need pain and suffering to fully comprehend the meaning of hope, and that the gateway between the two is forgiveness; that through pain we understand more fully how to trust, and that this makes the concept of hope more vivid and real.

Hope is nothing if it doesn't exist when all seems hopeless. You have to experience fear, anxiety, pain, hopelessness to truly know what hope is. In the words of Václav Havel, who wrote a great deal on the theme of hope, 'perhaps hopelessness is the very soil that nourishes human hope'.[10] We have to inhabit the fear and suffering of Good Friday and dwell with it, to fully experience the hope and joy of Easter resurrection. And the place where we encounter the beginnings of hope is right here at the foot of the cross as we gaze on the body of our Lord, arms outstretched, crying 'Father, forgive'.

Prayer

Forgiving God,
when the world condemns us, when wrong is done to us, when we carry the weight of things that are too much to forgive, come alongside us in the darkness, and give us the grace to be forgiven and to forgive. Amen.

'Today you will be with me in Paradise'

2

'Today you will be with me in Paradise'

One of the criminals who were hanged there kept deriding him and saying, 'Are you not the Messiah? Save yourself and us!' But the other rebuked him, saying, 'Do you not fear God, since you are under the same sentence of condemnation? And we indeed have been condemned justly, for we are getting what we deserve for our deeds, but this man has done nothing wrong.' Then he said, 'Jesus, remember me when you come into your kingdom.' He replied, 'Truly I tell you, today you will be with me in Paradise.'

Luke 23.39–43

I confess I feel a special affinity towards this second saying of Jesus from the cross, directed towards the criminal hanging next to him, and it's purely sentimental: 'today you will be with me in paradise.' In part I'm drawn to it because the word 'paradise' is originally a Persian word and has its roots in my culture and tradition. It's amazing how significant it can be to see elements of ourselves reflected within Scripture: characters, places or words that reveal something of our own experiences. Perhaps that's why minority groups who traditionally haven't had much say in interpreting the Bible find it so powerful to read

Scripture from their own particular perspective – to read themselves back into the story of God and God's people, where often they've been airbrushed out, ignored or made invisible.

But back to the word 'paradise'. In Jewish and Christian traditions, paradise is associated especially with the Garden of Eden, but in the New Testament it appears only three times – once here, in Jesus' words as presented in Luke, then in Paul's second letter to the Corinthians (12.4) and finally in the book of Revelation (2.7). The word conjures up the idea of an eastern oasis. Literally meaning 'an enclosed space' or 'that which grows in a designated space', the Persian Garden of Paradise is a walled-in garden apparently untouched by the severity of the desert landscape all around. It is a space in which wild, uncontrollable forces are tamed and cultivated according to certain rules and strict symmetries. A paradise garden will always include elements of shade, significant water features, and will be enhanced by fruit trees and sweet-scented flowers.

So Jesus' promise of paradise is comforting partly because it reconnects me with my roots. It touches my soul in a way I can't really explain. The image is one of safety and protection, beauty and peace. But it is neither schmaltzy nor saccharine, for it points also to the reality of the desert all around – the wilderness that is never far away, just beyond the protective walls. Paradise Gardens wouldn't have the power and impact they do if they didn't sit in such stark contrast to the surrounding landscape. Stepping into a Paradise Garden takes the breath away, in part because of its close proximity to the arid and barren countryside within touching distance of the lush, green and fertile enclosure. The power of the imagery lies in the contrast between the two, each more potent because of the other. In fact you cannot really have a Paradise Garden in the proper sense without the wasteland that surrounds it.

And, of course, the ideas of both paradise and desert or wilderness are central themes in Christianity and the story of our faith – and here we're confronted by them as we contemplate the cross of Christ. A little like forgiveness in Chapter 1, which sits alongside the call for justice, I want to suggest that the ideas of paradise and desert go hand in hand. Apparently total opposites, they inform one another, each giving meaning to the other and making our experience fuller and more complete. And even more than that, it is perfectly possible to encounter glimpses of paradise from the heartlands of the desert.

The cross is the ultimate wilderness, where God's presence seems utterly absent in the face of unimaginable suffering and inevitable death. Surely we can't imagine a place of greater loneliness and emptiness, where evil is all around and God is silent. Where, I wonder, are these places in your life? So much hurt and brokenness, so much anger and bitterness that even God cannot penetrate? And yet it is from that very place that Jesus says to the criminal, 'today you will be with me in paradise.' This isn't an insincere 'All will be well – just stick it out for a while' offered from the sidelines. This is Jesus reaching out from his own place of pain, from the very heart of his own desert experience – a reminder of God's presence even here, even now. You are not alone, if only you can see it.

Jesus' wounds as he suffers on the cross are wounds filled with promise of healing – healing that can come only from one who has experienced deep woundedness himself. This is the place, hanging on the cross, where Jesus becomes Christ the wounded healer. He is both suffering humanity and divine healer, and what he offers isn't a vision of something far away but something here and now, for paradise is imminent: '*today* you will be with me in paradise.' Throughout his earthly life, in each 'today' in which so many different people encountered Jesus, that encounter brought salvation: it brought healing; it brought restoration; it brought wholeness. Even now in his hour of death he extends salvation to the one who seeks it. There is immediacy: 'Come,' he says, 'let's step into it together' – paradise is here, even in this place of death, pain mingled with blessing, each sanctifying the other.

We can only imagine what life-events had enslaved the criminal hanging next to Jesus – what sadnesses and betrayals, what desert experiences of his own. But on the cross, just as he is paying for his sins, he is invited from bondage to freedom. There are echoes here of the Israelites led from slavery in Egypt towards freedom in the promised land. *That* freedom had brought with it 40 years in the wilderness – a lifetime for many of them – where they often doubted God's presence and felt sure they had been duped and left literally deserted. They longed sometimes to return to the safety of what they knew, even if it was the safety of oppression and servitude. Better that than the emptiness they now experienced.

But the point is that God was always present in the wilderness, whether the Israelites recognised it or not. The promise of the covenant God made with them meant they were never forsaken. And yet even as they crossed the red sea, as they gathered manna to eat, as they built false idols to worship, again and again they failed to notice God in the desert in their very midst – paradise *ever present* while they strained to catch a glimpse of it somewhere in the distance.

As I reflect on my own experience of exodus – my journey from a place of revolution and danger to a place of safety – I recognise both wilderness and paradise. It's now over 40 years since I arrived in England – 40 years in the wilderness you might say. Like the Israelites, I didn't expect it to be for so long, imagining we would be back home within a few weeks or months, a year at most. Casting my mind back now, I see the young teenager packing her suitcase, trying to decide what to take and what to leave; I see her saying goodbye to friends, exchanging hugs and small gifts; I see her looking out of the aeroplane at the desert plains of Iran, not fully comprehending what was happening; I see her learning to navigate a new culture and embrace a new beginning, find a kind of homecoming, a paradise in the wilderness. And yes it was lonely, and yes there is deep yearning to return home, almost a physical ache to touch and see and smell the places of my childhood (which will of course have changed beyond recognition), to reconnect with roots and simply dwell awhile.

And there are many like me – so many people displaced. And many, *many* have it so much worse than I ever did. Conditions are much tougher now for refugees and asylum seekers, governments stricter and people more suspicious. Many risk life and limb trying to find their paradise, use all their savings – worse still, are stripped of their dignity. Some, of course, never make it: children, women and men who don't survive the journey and others who get separated from loved ones or whose paradise turns out to be a refugee camp or a detention centre.

The evils that humanity brings upon itself; the deserts we create through war and greed and our inability to cope with difference and diversity. How can we possibly talk of salvation and paradise amid such horrors and inhumanities? Who am I to claim that God is present and Christ is reaching out with promise of deliverance for those whose suffering is beyond comprehension? We are, it seems, utterly impotent, and yet in that impotence, in our very helplessness, our gaze is drawn towards the cross and we look with bewilderment on the one who hangs there – the one who turns upside down all our notions of what it means to be powerful, successful or wise; the one who shows us that it *is* possible to bring good out of evil, to transform death to life, to find strength in vulnerability. And there, as we look and as we contemplate, little by little we gain strength to work for change – not just a promise of paradise for tomorrow but commitment to work for paradise today, here and now, transforming lives; co-workers with the God of love.

'Today you will be with me in paradise', Jesus said to the criminal who hadn't actually repented of his sins, hadn't asked for clemency and didn't expect anything from Jesus other than the hope of being remembered – 'remember me when you come into your kingdom'. To be remembered is perhaps the greatest thing we can hope for. When we've gone and there's nothing left of us but memories, the greatest achievement will be to be remembered by loved ones from time to time. That remembrance gives life again, for a few moments at a time. But Jesus offers so much more, freely and with no expectations in return. The gift of faith allows us to recognise paradise even in the driest of desert places – to notice love in the midst of pain, good in the midst of evil, kindness in the midst of hatred.

And faith enables us to reach out and take the saviour's hand in trust. This is neither mirage nor hallucination. It is a gift offered to all, and it comes from the cross of Christ.

Prayer

Reconciling God,
we are weighed down by sin and separation, a world that is not at peace, people who are not whole. Your son Jesus Christ reached out to the thief and welcomed him out of the desert into your paradise. Come alongside us in the darkness, and bring grace and peace to everything that is broken. Amen.

3

'Here is your son ...
here is your mother'

3

'Here is your son ...
here is your mother'

Meanwhile, standing near the cross of Jesus were his mother, and his mother's sister, Mary the wife of Clopas, and Mary Magdalene. When Jesus saw his mother and the disciple whom he loved standing beside her, he said to his mother, 'Woman, here is your son.' Then he said to the disciple, 'Here is your mother.' And from that hour the disciple took her into his own home.

John 19.25–27

A couple of years ago I heard Paul Boateng speak, passionately and emotively, about the racism he's experienced over the years as a black man in politics. Despite the shocking and abhorrent stories he shared, Boateng suggested that *identity* is an even bigger issue than race – consuming our imagination and requiring careful attention. Identity, I agree, is a major preoccupation of our times. Consciously or subconsciously, many people are on a quest to discover and articulate who they are, how they belong and where they fit in. As well as the mass movement of displaced people globally, migrants and refugees who search for roots in new and foreign lands, there's been the small matter of Brexit, which has led to questions about European versus British identity, not to mention the distinct identities of the four nations of the United Kingdom.

Then there's the explosion of identity politics that has grown out of new and complex ways of understanding sexuality and gender, expressing disparity not so much in binary terms but more as a spectrum of diversity. Ironically, instead of diminishing the significance of the things that divide us, identity politics appears to have bred a whole new set of fault lines. Individuals seek a sense of belonging in ever more specific groupings, often defined in quite dogmatic terms over and against others. But also, since the affluence and wealth of the latter part of the twentieth century, many in the West have come to realise that their priorities have perhaps been misplaced, and they are now searching for a more real identity – something above and beyond the material and physical to give meaning to their lives.

For myself, I'm fascinated by the concept of identity and how it ties in with my sense of belonging. I suppose it's hardly surprising, given my life story and the rupture from my homeland at the impressionable age of 14, in somewhat traumatic circumstances. I feel sometimes that I was robbed of a proper sense of belonging, destined instead to exist somewhere in nowhere land. But if I'm honest, the roots of the dilemma go back much further, to when I was even younger, growing up as a Christian in Iran. The tiny Anglican Church there was made up of a mixture of converts, second-generation Christians like myself and foreign missionaries. Ours was an odd existence by any standards, and in truth we never quite fitted in.

Our context was a missionary church seeking to develop its own identity with an authentically Persian voice, within an environment where *national* identity was overwhelmingly regarded as coterminous with *religious* identity.

In the West, faith is generally thought of as a personal matter, whereas in the East it is deeply rooted in one's culture, racial ties and heritage – faith strikes at the very core of one's social and national identity. In Iran, to be Persian was to be Muslim, and specifically Shi'a Muslim. To not be Muslim was regarded as a kind of betrayal of your nationality, raising all sorts of questions about your identity, who you were and how you fitted in. For the Church, the challenge was how to be both authentically Christian *and* fully Persian. For me, especially in my adult life as I've reflected on my own past and how it's shaped me, there's been a quest to discover who I am and how I fit in.

So whether growing up in Iran or finding my place in this country, there's a sense in which I've always been a stranger and interloper, living with the ever-present anxiety of just not quite fitting in. The challenge has been to not get stuck in that place which is neither one thing nor another – not to sit on the boundaries with the wallowing self-pity of an outsider, but to be more creative, transforming my experience of being on the margins from something that defines me negatively into a positive place full of richness, meaning and hope.

Some years ago, I read a novel by Anne Tyler called *Digging to America*.[11] It had a powerful impact on me and remains with me to this day. The book is about two families in America, each of whom adopts a baby girl from Korea. The extended families meet at the airport as the two girls are delivered into their care, and the remainder of the book is about how their lives intertwine. Very little happens by way of plot, but underlying the narrative are questions about identity, displacement and belonging. Though the nationality of the girls themselves is relevant, more crucial to the story is that one of the families has migrated from, as it happens, Iran. You have this extraordinary encounter between American and Iranian identities seeking to incorporate aspects of Korean culture into their lives.

Tyler expertly and movingly narrates how a Persian family in exile is struggling to belong in a foreign country. The Iranian grandmother, Maryam, remains with me vividly. As the story unfolds we see her struggle, wanting to be accepted as a regular American while at the same time resisting it. She feels that Americans will never understand her, that their interest in her is patronising and condescending. And, of course, deep down she's anxious to remain true to her own culture and roots, frightened that assimilation would result in loss of her identity as an Iranian. But in her struggle she's sinking ever deeper into a lonely place – a kind of vacuum where she's utterly displaced and doesn't in fact belong anywhere.

A moment of epiphany comes when Maryam finally realises that *she herself* is blocking the path to belonging. She has hardened her heart towards her host nation and its people. She has dwelt on that which is different, and used their alien ways to judge them. She has undermined the common humanity that binds them together by dwelling on her own otherness. Maryam finally realises that she cannot remain encased in her own heritage, which is already displaced from its geographical roots and therefore something different from what it once was. Rather, she must move into the future and embrace a new way of belonging. She must be generous to others and willing to receive from those who want to be generous to her. Maryam finally recognises her choice either to remain entrapped by self-pity or reach out in friendship so that those who are different can travel together, and learn about each other and themselves in the process.

Maryam will of course always be different and will probably continue to struggle with questions of identity. But the point is, by seeing goodness in the motives of others and by recognising her need of their friendship, she escapes an additional *self-imposed* burden that deliberately places her on the outside. In other words, *you have to want to belong*. It's not something that will happen on its own. You have to give birth to it, work at it and create it through an intentional act of the will.

And what was true for Maryam is true for me and I believe all of us to some extent. However much it may appear that we belong and fit in perfectly, and however much we play the game pretending that we do, in reality many of us feel we are somehow different, for a whole variety of reasons. Very few have a sense of belonging completely. The question is, do we wallow in that, judge others and position ourselves on the boundaries – find reasons why we're different, why we don't fit in, why the rules don't apply to us? Or can we make peace with our past and with our roots, and with all the complexity within us, accept these as part of who we are and find new ways of belonging? Can we dwell not on what divides us from others but on those common albeit fragile threads of humanity that bring us together?

And so at last we attend to Jesus' cry from the cross to his mother Mary and the disciple whom he loved – 'here is your son' he says to Mary, and to John 'here is your mother'. In his agony and moment of absolute isolation – the point at which his identity is in the balance, his humanity and divinity struggling to assert themselves – Jesus releases Mary and John from the tight hold of what has been familiar and safe. In an extraordinary act of generosity, Jesus loosens the bonds of their familial ties, lightens the weight of their histories and eases the stranglehold of the stories that had brought each of them to this place. He gives permission for a new future and points them towards a new way of belonging, which is less about their own preoccupations and more about the potential of new relationships through him; less concerned with tradition and history and individuality and more concerned with exploration, connectedness and community.

When I was in my late twenties and early thirties, my husband and I experienced many years of infertility. After extensive treatment, two miscarriages and much heartache we were granted the gift of children. I remember well when my first child was finally born. It felt like the whole world was rejoicing with me, that I'd been blessed with a longed-for gift, my prayers and deepest longings fulfilled. I confess, it was many years before I began to understand that it wasn't really about me at all; that although my joy was – and remains – deep, the children are not here primarily for my fulfilment. They are here to live their own lives, to discover their own purpose, to grow and move and find their being in the God who loves them and desires good things for them. I may have given birth to them, and for good and ill I've had a part to play in their evolving stories, but ultimately they must each discover their own identity and place of belonging as separate from me.

Of course our roots are important and of course our families help to shape us and give us a sense of place in the world. But the point is that we don't need to be constrained by the boundaries within which life seeks to encase us. For through this third word from the cross, we're encouraged to look wider, higher and deeper than those borders that confine us to narrow ways of belonging. Whoever you are, wherever you come from, whatever your story, there is a common identity that binds us all as children of God, each uniquely made in the divine image and loved as part of the glorious diversity of creation.

At Christ's death on the cross, everything that constrains our humanity is thrown into question. Power is made manifest through weakness, authority is demonstrated through sacrifice, and death becomes the moment of glory. And so we can discover ourselves anew. As Jesus recognises the pain of Mary and John, so our suffering and pain too is recognised and we are released to become a new creation. Our stories are important but they need not define us.

This mysterious complexity is what my sisters and I have tried to capture on our parents' gravestone, where they are buried, far from their homeland, in a patch of ground – fittingly called 'Paradise' – on the south-eastern side of Winchester Cathedral. On one side of the grave are carved words in English, *Dust of the high plains of Persia in the earth of an English shire.* And on the other side, in Persian, are words from St Paul's letter to the Ephesians (2.19), 'So then you are no longer strangers and foreigners, but fellow citizens with the saints, and members of God's household.'

Prayer

Loving God,
we carry the imprint of the people we love, and the stories
that have shaped us. Our past is part of who we are, and
sometimes it prevents us from moving on. Come alongside
us in the darkness, and free us to become all that you want
us to be. Amen.

4

'My God, my God,
why have you forsaken me?'

4

'My God, my God, why have you forsaken me?'

When it was noon, darkness came over the whole land until three in the afternoon. At three o'clock Jesus cried out with a loud voice, 'Eloi, Eloi, lema sabachthani?' which means, 'My God, my God, why have you forsaken me.' When some of the bystanders heard it, they said, 'Listen, he is calling for Elijah.' And someone ran, filled a sponge with sour wine, put it on a stick, and gave it to him to drink, saying, 'Wait, let us see whether Elijah will come to take him down.' Then Jesus gave a loud cry and breathed his last. And the curtain of the temple was torn in two, from top to bottom. Now when the centurion, who stood facing him, saw that in this way he breathed his last, he said, 'Truly this man was God's Son!'

Mark 15.33–39

One of my abiding memories of the early days of the Revolution in Iran is the suddenness with which the Church community found itself alone and isolated. There were weeks, if not months, during which things were increasingly unsettled and chaotic. Curfew was in place, schools were closed, there were daily demonstrations, with a feeling of growing uncertainty creeping across the country. But for me, and others as well I think, there was one moment in which the reality sank in that everything seemed to have changed. I can't remember the precise date or timeline, though I suspect it was in the lead-up to Christmas 1979. One weekend there was a performance of Handel's *Messiah* in church – given by a mixed group of missionaries and other foreigners, with some local Christians also participating. I think my eldest sister and brother were probably involved. The church was full to bursting. But by the following weekend, when we were once again in church, they were all gone. Just like that. The mission society and other foreign organisations had pulled out all their people, judging it too dangerous to allow them to stay. The change was abrupt and dramatic. Suddenly, in an increasingly hostile environment, our tiny community felt very vulnerable and exposed.

These words of Jesus from the cross remind me of that time. 'My God, my God, why have you forsaken me?' They express something of the sheer aloneness of Jesus, abandoned by the people and most of his disciples, in a place of fear and pain, nearing the end of his life. He struggles to breathe and writhes in agony, and feels abandoned even by God. There is nothing. He is utterly alone.

So here, it seems, we encounter the absence of God. And we dwell in that absence, amid loneliness and fear. There is nowhere else to go and no one to turn to. We have no choice but to wait – to stay and to abide. And as we did exactly that in Iran, we had to face the reality of the situation, of who we really were as a community, fragile and vulnerable, without anyone or anything to hide behind. There were no outsiders to make us feel a little safer; there was no escape and nothing to conceal us. The future was uncertain, but although we didn't know it, there was worse to come – arrest and imprisonment for some, the murder of my brother, and eventually exile for us as a family.

Many of you will have faced places of fear and abandonment, perhaps through illness, grief, unemployment, divorce, homelessness and for all sorts of other reasons; will have faced those times when despite how our modern western culture leads us to believe that we can control every detail of our lives, in truth we are sometimes powerless and have no control. All we're left with is our weakness, frailty and vulnerability. At such times we have no choice but to face who we are, in the cold light of day or the dark loneliness of the night, when even God feels far away or absent. It's then we begin to understand that what we *do* in life counts for little; that our skills, gifts and abilities – the things we thought we could control – are pretty meaningless, for they cannot save us or pull us out of the pit of abandonment. All the things that used to give shape and meaning to our lives suddenly count for very little, and what we are left with is the essence of who we *are*, naked, as it were, before our maker.

I have a friend who's struggling with a disease that's gradually disabling her body. It's a degenerative muscular condition that over time is depriving her of the things she used to take for granted, and causing her considerable physical pain. She is gifted and creative and was destined for senior posts of considerable responsibility. As she's stripped of the things she felt gave her a purpose and value and recognition, she is having to reconsider her worth as a child of God, not in terms of *what she does* but of *who she is*. It is very painful, and it comes to all of us in old age if not sooner – letting go of the things we once considered essential to our self-understanding.

How do we find self-worth when we can't rely on the things that give us status and our place in society? Henri Nouwen, who after many years as a priest and academic went to live in the Daybreak Community, where able-bodied and disabled people live alongside each other, soon realised that among those with mental disabilities, his achievements as a theologian, writer and scholar counted for nothing. Nouwen had to emerge from the place of abandonment and rediscover the core of his humanity, which had nothing to do with his skills and everything to do with the nature of his relationships.[12]

I see something similar happen to those who are refugees, many of whom were highly qualified professionals in their home country. Doctors, engineers and architects, for example, find themselves in exile, unable to use their considerable skills, often not allowed to work at all. How do you hang on to a sense of who you are when you're stripped of the things you do? The pain and the agony aside, that's where Jesus was on the cross – totally powerless and alone, no more miracles or fine sermons with which to impress the crowds, no disciples hanging on his every word, no longer even the presence of God to reassure and to encourage. Remember the words at his baptism resonating for all to hear: 'You are my Son, the Beloved; with you I am well pleased' (Mark 1.11)? – no trace or echo of that now, only silence and emptiness.

And yet this lowest point is also the point of greatest glory. For the shame and weakness of the cross reveal something of the nature of Jesus (who of course mirrors the nature of God), and that nature is an outpouring of love so strong that it submits even to death on the cross. It will be apparent to you by now that I rely on paradoxes to aid me in my faith journey – all those many apparent contradictions that must be held together in tension, challenging us to reside in the 'in-between' spaces of life and faith, without the luxury of simplistic black-and-white answers: the God who unsettles yet gives peace beyond understanding; the God who demands justice but is endlessly forgiving; the God who loves beyond measure but appears to abandon us in our greatest hours of need.

And here, of course, is perhaps the greatest paradox of all. The death of Jesus, his moment of complete abandonment, becomes also his moment of greatest glory, for through faithfulness – the offering of himself once and for all – his weakness becomes his strength as he overturns the power of violence and hatred, replacing them with compassion and love. And here's the thing: when we are in our places of abandonment, hanging on our crosses, alone and powerless, we too share in that glory. This is not easy and it's not some feeble cliché.

I certainly don't mean to underestimate the extent of suffering in our world nor minimise the importance of speaking and acting against injustice. There is far too much suffering and far too much injustice, and some people have way more than their fair share of them. Striving towards creating the kingdom of God here on earth means that we are compelled to do our part in working for change. But – and here's the paradox again – when all is said and done, in our moments of pain and anguish, loneliness and abandonment, our suffering takes us closer to the heart of God, for it gives us insights into the person of Christ, deepening our trust and faith.

At the height of the Revolution in Iran, my father wrote these words, which I still have on a poster that hangs on my study wall:

> The way of the cross has suddenly become so meaning-ful that we have willingly walked in it with our Lord near us. Our numbers have become smaller, our earthly supports have gone, but we are learning the meaning of faith in a new and deeper way.[13]

Jesus' cry of abandonment from the cross is a call to dwell sometimes in the place of pain; to recognise the reality and the horror; to understand that nothing and no one can help change the situation, that there is no light, only darkness; but to know too that Jesus himself has been in that very place and that we are nearest to him precisely when we may feel furthest away. Our pain connects with his pain – he understands and can redeem our moments of despair and aloneness, for through them we come to understand that our strength in fact lies in how we accept our weakness, in how we are when we're at our lowest ebb. It's not until you squeeze an orange and release its juice that you find out if it is bitter or sweet. It's not until we are wounded and hurt that we discover what is really within us, whether it is a capacity for hate or love, fear or hope.

I'm not sure that God was absent when Jesus cried out in despair. Rather, I wonder if God was simply silent – silent because there was nothing left to say in the face of the horror that was the cross. Have you ever sat with a friend who is in deep grief at the loss of a loved one, or held the hand of someone waiting for major surgery? Have you ever embraced a child who has fallen and hurt themselves, listened to the life story of a prisoner or wept with a refugee or homeless person? If you have done any of these things or something like them, you will know that feeling of being lost for words. There is nothing you can say to help. Only silence will do; it's all that is left.

So as Christ hangs on the cross crying 'why have you forsaken me?', has God turned away because he cannot bear to look, or is she lovingly present but voiceless? Either way, God has no answer to the depth of human suffering; and that's what we witness here. There is no divine response, only silence – it is the loudest silence of all and painful to hear. But it is a silence that envelops and carries us through grace and disgrace; in the words of the contemporary contemplative Martin Laird, a silence that 'presides in the unfolding liturgy of our wounds'.[14]

Prayer

Ever present God,
your son Jesus knows what it is to feel far from you. We are sometimes bowed down by the weight of your silence. Come alongside us in the darkness, and help us to recognise your presence with us. Amen.

5

'I thirst'

5

'I thirst'

After this, when Jesus knew that all was now finished,
he said (in order to fulfil the scripture), 'I am thirsty.' A
jar full of sour wine was standing there. So they put a
sponge full of the wine on a branch of hyssop and held
it to his mouth.

John 19.28–29

If you know anything about Iran you will know that it
is a vast country, roughly eight times the size of Great
Britain. Its 636,000 square miles include an extensive central desert region and formidable mountain ranges that
separate towns and cities on every side – an inhospitable
environment where very little survives in the extreme
temperatures and arid climate. I remember well the long
car journeys as a child – seven or eight hours in any
direction from Isfahan, where we lived, towards Tehran,
Shiraz, Yazd and other places. Long before the days of
mobile phones, we would leave early in the morning – at
3 or 4 a.m. – to ensure we were well on the way before
the worst of the heat. You could drive for miles and miles
and see nothing but a brown landscape and the long road
stretching out ahead – sometimes cut through the sheer
rock face, with what was left towering on either side;
other times with the level wilderness all around, as far as
the eye could see.

Stops had to be planned carefully at the few watering holes or caravanserais along the way. Cups of sweet black tea, flat bread with cheese and walnuts, slices of watermelon always tasted better on these journeys. Punctures were a serious hazard and the risk of running out of water a real one. I was oblivious to the dangers as a child and remember only the sense of excitement, anticipation and, after we'd been on the road for a few hours, boredom; but now I realise how vulnerable we were and how exposed to the potential risks all around.

As we enter the final stages of our vigil at the foot of the cross, we hear Jesus utter the two simple words 'I thirst', thereby exposing his vulnerability and ultimately his *humanity*. If we have any doubt that the son of God came down to earth and took human form, then here that doubt is expelled. Jesus is thirsty. Here the story of the cross becomes our story, for the terrible story of the one who is falsely accused, abandoned by friends, stripped, humiliated, who cries out in pain and desolation, is also the beautiful story of God who came to earth to share our humanity.

Just a few hours earlier in the Garden of Gethsemane, Jesus had prayed to the Father; had implored him to let this cup pass from him. But now, here on the cross, he's ready to embrace the calling at the heart of his ministry – he claims the cup the Father has given him. 'I thirst', he says, and reaches out towards what lies ahead. In this 'I thirst', Jesus' resistance ends – he surrenders and accepts his vocation, which is to overcome the power of evil and hatred by giving himself in love. This poses a question and indeed a challenge for us all. What is your vocation and have you embraced it? Are you *doing* and *being* what you are called to do and be? Are you able to say 'I thirst', knowing it may be costly and painful but also that drinking the cup is the only way to fulfil your particular vocation – the only way to true fulfilment and to being the person God intends you to be?

As Jesus clasps the cup it seems that he is totally alone, but in acknowledging his humanity he is also indicating his reliance on those around him. Alone he cannot quench his thirst – he needs others to put the sponge to his lips. Even the Son of Man requires assistance. And underlying this is the extraordinary truth that God needs our co-operation: without us, God's plans for the world cannot come to fruition. If God's kingdom is to come on earth, we must play our part in both smaller and larger ways, working for peace and justice in our homes, churches, communities, our country and our world. And not one of us is self-sufficient. Despite the illusion of control, despite both our reluctance to admit to weakness and frailty and our desire to seem omni-competent, none of us – even the strongest – can survive alone. We need one another. There are times when we must ask for help and admit to failure and brokenness.

Some are better at recognising this than others, better at modelling our interconnectedness and reliance on one another. And it has been my experience that when we are able to expose our weaknesses and frailties, rather than limiting or diminishing us, those very imperfections become the means by which we connect with others at a deeper level, allowing them in turn to recognise their frailty. Each link forged in this way adds to the chain that is the bond of our humanity; each link drives us towards greater compassion and gentleness for one another.

We haven't dwelt too much yet on the sheer physicality of the crucifixion, on the brutality of death on a cross, the unimaginable strain that it put on the body, the long, slow and agonising death. But let's make no bones about it: it was a cruel and truly dreadful way to die. The simple cry of 'I thirst' doesn't begin to capture the full extent of the horror, but it does contain within it something of the frailty of the human condition and our need of others' support.

When we first arrived in England in May of 1980, we had very little by way of worldly goods – just one suitcase each, which we had packed in the few days between my brother's murder, his funeral and our departure. We were totally reliant on the good will and generosity of others. But we were fortunate – we had family who took us in, and in time the church structures kicked in to provide us with a base from which to rebuild our lives. I never heard my parents complain and I know they felt deep gratitude, but I also remember sensing that it wasn't always easy for them to accept charity, to admit they were no longer self-sufficient but at the mercy of others.

For some reason the memory of a blunt potato peeler has remained with me. It was in a box along with various other kitchen utensils that someone had cleared out of their home and brought round as a gift. As we struggled to peel vegetables later that day, my mother, in her gentle way, wondered what use someone imagined she might have for a blunt peeler that really needed throwing out. In his hour of need, when Jesus cried out 'I thirst', it was sour wine he was offered on a sponge – hardly a drink to quench his thirst, I imagine, though perhaps it made the person offering it feel a little better. At least they were doing something. But charity shouldn't just be about doing anything to salve our conscience. It should be a gracious offering – costly even – coming from the best of what we have.

My mind turns once more to those who are refugees today – the hundreds and thousands who have been displaced and forced to leave their homelands, many having faced untold dangers getting here and perhaps lost loved ones along the way; those professionals who have left good jobs and spent their life-savings to reach safety; those who had nothing in the first place, arriving here destitute and alone; those held in detention centres, whose cases take months or years to be heard, who aren't allowed to work and who receive meagre benefits that aren't enough to live on; those stripped of their dignity. Each one has a story to tell, each echoing Christ's 'I thirst', which in the end is the cry of all humanity. For ultimately very little separates us from one another. Very little lies between those who have and those who have not, those who belong and those who feel they don't – a handful of unforeseen circumstances, the odd bit of bad luck. How would I respond to another's cry of 'I thirst' if I truly understood that what unites us is far greater than what divide us; that we all thirst and all need help to quench that thirst?

That is what I see demonstrated in social-action projects that work with refugees. Not so long ago I visited Leicester City of Sanctuary, which seeks to offer a warm welcome and practical support for asylum seekers and refugees – there are many Cities of Sanctuary across the UK. I spent several hours talking with those who work there, providing everything from a cooked meal, sewing and English classes, to massages and football for the children. I also

47

listened to the stories of those seeking asylum in this country – several were from Iran, delighted to meet someone they could talk to in their own language. But what struck me wasn't so much that some people had come for help and others were offering it, but that *together* they were cooperating and collaborating – refugees, asylum seekers and British citizens all contributing through cooking, running stalls, playing with the children, all giving of their time and, crucially, all gaining something through their encounter with one another.

Several volunteers told me how much they enjoy being there and how much they benefit from the experience. This is a model that has very little to do with some people giving from a place of abundance to others who come empty handed, and much more to do with getting alongside one another, each recognising the worth of the other, each contributing to and benefitting from the other. And in the process, each discovers that all of us thirst and all of us need to help quench the thirst of others. This is at the core of our humanity and it is a recognition that to *belong* we need to feel we are *contributing*.

And when we truly feel we belong – that we are both contributing to and being cared for by others – then we also have a sense of purpose, which in turn gives hope and the possibility to imagine a better future. In Jesus' cry of 'I thirst', I detect something of the deep human instinct for choosing life over death. He was so near the end and yet he hadn't given up – he longs for change; even at this late stage he believes in the possibility of transformation. When we reach that point in life when all seems hopeless and we are totally overwhelmed – when we are burdened by anxiety, guilt, loss, shame, fear, pain or anger – then the cry of 'I thirst' prevents us reaching the point of no return. It is an acknowledgement that I may need the help of others but that I long for change and transformation.

The denial of emptiness within us will not do. Our brokenness cannot be buried, erased or forgotten but it can, with help and by God's grace, be transformed. Desolation can turn to consolation, and even the most difficult of situations can be turned to good. For that is the power of the cross, turning violence to gentleness, hatred to love and death to life. Shortly, a soldier will pierce Jesus' side to make sure he's dead before his body is removed from the cross. As the sword penetrates his body, we are told, blood and water gush out. This has been no ordinary death, the crucifixion of some unfortunate criminal. This is the son of God, an innocent man, fulfilling his vocation and turning all the norms of the world upside down. This is the thirsty one who is also the bearer of life-giving water; whose broken body becomes the bread of life, whose blood becomes the cup of salvation. This is the wounded healer whose suffering shows us the extent of God's love for us.

He embraces pain not because it is good in itself but as a means of absorbing the suffering that is part of the way of the world. And he beckons us to follow his example – to use our wounds to become those who are not bowed down, bitter and angry, but those who reach out in compassion to others. For our suffering takes us closer to the heart of God who knows and understands the pain and who gives us strength to become life-bearers as well as being those who thirst.

Prayer

Dependable God,
in all our thirst, and all our longing, in all our failure and
all our devotion, you are there. Come alongside us in
the darkness, and walk with us through all our anguish.
Amen.

6 & 7

*'It is finished' …
'Into your hands, O Lord,
I commend my spirit'*

6 & 7

'It is finished' ...
'Into your hands, O Lord,
I commend my spirit'

*When Jesus had received the wine, he said, 'It is finished.'
Then he bowed his head and gave up his spirit.*

John 19.30

*It was now about noon, and darkness came over the
whole land until three in the afternoon, while the sun's
light failed; and the curtain of the temple was torn in
two. Then Jesus, crying with a loud voice, said, 'Father,
into your hands I commend my spirit.' Having said this,
he breathed his last.*

Luke 23.44–46

Here are two sayings rolled into one. As he nears the end
of his ordeal, Jesus cries 'it is finished' and 'into your hands
I commend my spirit'. For me, underlying these final two
utterances from the cross are three distinct but intercon-
nected themes. First, a hollow and devastating expression
of total loss: it is finished, it's all over; and in the emptiness there are echoes of defeat, and there is grief for what
might have been – a miscarried opportunity. It may sound
shocking, but I don't think it's unreasonable to hear in
Jesus' 'it is finished' something of that overwhelming sense

53

of meaninglessness many of us can associate with, and perhaps too a hint of relief that at least the pain is almost past; whatever it was, the worst is nearly over. I have sympathy for that – it seems like a very real human emotion, and one we shouldn't deny our saviour.

And yet that is not the full extent of it. 'It is finished' contains within it the human cry of despair, but it is also – and this is my second theme – a shout of triumph at the completion of a task, expression of a real sense of achievement. I've done it! I've done what you called me to do, Jesus says to his Father, and I've done it faithfully. The cry is equivalent to the athlete's punch in the air at the end of a marathon. Yes, I've made it, I'm over the line – I've accomplished what you sent me to do, I've fulfilled my calling and I couldn't have done any more.

Behind this lies something that I learnt from my parents as I watched them adjust to exile and the loss, in human terms at least, of all they had devoted their lives to in Iran. The Church they had served, which had its roots in the missionary movement but had striven to become its own authentically Persian witness, was arguably an experiment that had failed. What little life it had left was being squeezed out of it, and it wasn't unreasonable to regard it as finished. But at least the worst was over (as far as my parents were concerned), and now they could turn their back on it and get on with the rest of their lives. And yet they refused to live as people who had been defeated, but remained instead hope-filled. They lived as those who had followed their calling and knew they could have done no more. Over the years there were, I'm sure, moments of darkness and doubt when they felt the stab of the nails that kept Christ hanging on the cross, the piercing of his side with a sword – the triumphant 'it is finished' barely a whisper on their lips. But they held fast and continued to offer their lives, in a whole new way, to serve the Church in Iran from exile. Thus exile was snatched out of the hands of failure and defeat, refusing to be identified merely as a place of banishment and loss, becoming instead a place of transformation, where new possibilities emerged and evil gave way to good.

And so the cry of anguish emanating from the cross, which is also the cry of completion and victory, gives way to another cry: 'it is finished' makes way for the prayer 'into your hands I commend my spirit'. When all is said and done, there is nothing left but to surrender to the will of God. And this submission is my third theme – letting go of all that has been in order to embrace that which lies ahead. This is not to forget or ignore or, worse still, deny the past; it is not a petulant refusal to participate any longer. It is, rather, an acknowledgement that there is only so much we can control. All through life, in different ways, small and large, there come times when we have to admit that we've done all we can. We've taken responsibility and played our part, and all that's left is to surrender, trusting God to use what has been – the good, the bad, the pain and the joy – and create out of it something that might bear fruit for the future.

Contemporary western society creates the illusion that we can control every aspect of our lives, shape outcomes and manipulate events to suit ourselves. But in truth we cannot be at peace until we learn the art of surrender. Whether it's creating the perfect family life, getting the longed-for job, managing our health, or whatever else we strive for, we can take responsibility and control up to a point (and it's right that we should), but eventually we must let go and let God. And as I reflect on life in exile, I can see that there has been a slow process of letting go – letting go of the past and of the person I was, in order to discover new things and become the person I was being called to be. Rather than clinging to the past in a futile attempt to recreate it in a new time and place, I have instead tried to acknowledge how the past has shaped and become part of me, while at the same time opening myself up to unexpected new possibilities for the future.

In March 2019 a service was held in Wakefield Cathedral to launch an authorised translation of the Church of England's Holy Communion service into Persian. This had come about in response to the growing number of Iranians turning up at churches across the country, eager to explore Christianity and in many cases to be baptised. Clergy and congregations have struggled over how best to offer a welcome. This translation not only provides the opportunity for Iranians to worship in their own language, but when laid out in parallel alongside the English, it allows people to worship together, each following the service in their own language but in a shared offering to God – a new intercultural experience.

Wakefield Cathedral was filled to the brim, standing room only, as this new creation was breathed into being. For many of the Iranians present – those who had come to faith in this country – this was the first time they were able to follow liturgy in their own language. For those of us present who remembered the Church in Iran and whose stories are bound up in its life and worship, there was great rejoicing – but if I'm honest, also some pain. This new embodiment of Persian Christianity is different from what I remember: not only are the words of the service somewhat changed from our version in Iran, but there are new songs and, at a deeper level, the emerging Persian-flavoured Christianity in the diaspora is different from ours in Iran. In Wakefield Cathedral, I was deeply conscious of the need for some of us to let go of something very dear in order to rejoice in the emergence of something new.

And the supreme example of that is presented to us by Christ on the cross – Christ who offers up all that he has been, lets go of the identity he has embodied on earth and surrenders to God through the pain of crucifixion, in order to become a new creation. It is not until a seed dies, buried deep within the darkness of the ground, that it issues forth new life. So it is with us. Not until we are willing to give up our grip on the old can something new emerge. But of course that new creation doesn't deny or nullify or eradicate what has been but is instead formed and shaped by it. The pain and suffering of the cross are carried into the resurrection when it comes, through the scars on Jesus' hands and side. The cross gives the resurrection its distinctive flavour – the new life that follows is coloured by its experience of death, so that it is not triumphalist, aggressive or grasping, but rather compassionate, gentle and long-suffering.

But that is not for now. Resurrection is still far off. Today we reside at the foot of the cross, witnesses to the crucifixion; we share in the death of Christ and it is here in the darkness that we must dwell. But as we watch and wait, so we too are shaped by the manner in which Christ bears his suffering, and we begin to open ourselves up, in all our loneliness, loss and pain, all our shame, regret and frailty; we open ourselves up to be transformed by his death, to become ever more compassionate and gentle as we embrace the new life we are offered.

Exile for me has been something like that – bearing the pain of loss but open to the possibility of transformation. And there is richness in the complexity, for it has given me insights into the suffering of others and allowed me to connect at a deep level with those who are far from home in so many different ways. All that I was (in what sometimes feels like a previous life), in all its beautiful messiness, informs what I have become and what I continue to become. For good and ill it has shaped me, and I have sought to offer it to God in its entirety, even as I have reached out towards that which is new, that which is unknown but continues to beckon me, the ongoing adventure of life and faith.

Each Good Friday we are given the opportunity to gaze for three hours at the cross of Christ and hear once more his seven last words. Whether or not we join in the hymns or appreciate the choir's sublime music, however helpful or unhelpful we find the reflections shared, whether we enjoy the silences or find them uncomfortable, there is no better place to be; no better way to spend those hours. It is only as we stop and take time to meditate on the cost of Christ's faithful sacrifice that we begin to get a glimpse of what it means to surrender our lives to God's will and, in so doing, discover who we really are as children of God, loved with a passion almost beyond comprehension.

Of course, such understanding requires us to see with the eyes of faith. Without faith the cross is nothing more than a gruesome and pointless death. And faith demands not certainty but a leap of trust and an open heart. There is no easy path to follow, nor are there easy answers to life's conundrums. The landscape of faith is a vast territory, stretching from certainty at one end to doubt at the other, through which we must navigate our way. Faith is an adventure that takes us to the darkest places, all the while offering just enough light to illuminate the way. Faith is at once both a journey into exile and a joyful homecoming – and it begins at the foot of the cross, from where we have heard the cries of one who understands our pain and journeys with us throughout.

Prayer

Compassionate God,
you rejoice in our faithfulness and you embrace us in our loneliness. When we mourn, when we are afraid, when we come to our own end, you are there too. Come alongside us in the darkness, and carry us through death to life. Amen.

The Tree of Knowledge

Having eaten only one fruit from it,
we cut the Tree of Knowledge down.

We broke its boughs, ripped it
from the land it fed and fed from.

Some man made branches with machines,
some woman cut new leaves from steel;

the tree sent up its sighs —

lamenting that the land it held together
could no longer now be held together.

From the tree's remains we made paper
but words kept on appearing on the pages
with warnings that we didn't want to read.

We burned it, dumped it, waited.
We wanted something else to save us.

© *Pádraig Ó Tuama, 2019*

Afterword from Holy Saturday

BY DAVID MONTEITH

Now there was a good and righteous man named Joseph, who, though a member of the council, had not agreed to their plan and action. He came from the Jewish town of Arimathea, and he was waiting expectantly for the kingdom of God. This man went to Pilate and asked for the body of Jesus. Then he took it down, wrapped it in a linen cloth, and laid it in a rock-hewn tomb where no one had ever been laid. It was the day of Preparation, and the sabbath was beginning. The women who had come with him from Galilee followed, and they saw the tomb and how his body was laid. Then they returned, and prepared spices and ointments. On the sabbath they rested according to the commandment.

Luke 23.50–56

Following on from Good Friday comes Holy Saturday. What is there to be said or what is there to be done after all the cries that come from the cross? These questions are intensified following the rich reflections in this book from a refugee bishop whose origins lie in a minority, persecuted Middle Eastern Church. Her Christian faith is shaped by the inheritance of western missionaries alongside indigenous contextualisation. This creates a faith biography that is full of pattern, texture, paradox and character. It is particular and timely. All the more reason to think there might be something to be said or to be done.

However, perhaps there is nothing to be said or done.

I remember preaching a three-hour meditation at St Martin-in-the-Fields similar in pattern to this written by Guli. As the bells rang at 3.00 p.m., I went out on to the portico of the church in search of air (somewhat polluted in central London), but asking myself that same question: What more is there to be said, or even has too much been said? And what is there to be done? I went for a walk through St James's Park, grumpily battling my way across a busy tourist-filled Trafalgar Square. People seemed apparently oblivious to the profundity of Good Friday, never mind my own personal journey with Jesus and my ache for some clarity in the light of being ever more convinced that 'God so loved the world' (John 3.16). These people presently in my way had been murmuring companions through the three hours as their voices bled into the church. Now they were in my face and in my ears, and they were far from serene. I needed space and silence and indeed no more words to process it all. Perhaps of all churches in London, St Martin's knows it is there for the world and for faith to make a difference in society. Yet here I was in the dilemma of working out what it is to walk in the way of the cross, to be a Good Friday people as the way to becoming an Easter people. How might the words and meditations of our hearts be not only acceptable to God but be offered as witness to a kingdom with a crucified king?

I knew that after all the drama of crucifixion was the silent ending of death, and it was hard to apprehend it, even having been with the story of Jesus for three hours. Quick on the heels of that Good Friday would be sunset, and the Saturday sabbath would begin with a body quickly prepared for a tomb. I once stood in the graveyard on the Mount of Olives, looking across the Kidron Valley over to Jerusalem, on a Friday afternoon as the sun started to set. Suddenly two cars pulled up full of Jewish men all bearing shovels, with a newly departed relative's body in the back of the car. As I watched them dig and bury, I understood for the first time the need for urgency following that Good Friday death of another Jewish man in Jerusalem. After the haste there would be a calm as the chill of death descended and the sun set.

Even at its most chaotic or dramatic, death brings its own quietude because there remains a body no longer animated with life but quickly changing colour to pallid hues. We focus in on things like a single spotlight at the end of a play just before curtains. Yet the bustle of the world continues round about, and the paradoxical coexistence of life and death remains hard to apprehend.

Recent experience has knocked that equilibrium as the world and climate have become more volatile. Death, disease and catastrophe don't seem so far away but much more close at hand. We've seen fire, famine and disease hit more places, including those in the northern hemisphere. In busy western life the tables are normally turned the other way round, with death and suffering squeezed to the margins as not part of our normal expectations of life but rather uncomfortable aliens in our very midst. However, power is shifting from north to south, and technology is unsettling everything from economics to understandings of nationhood. We find the deep disruption of threat, suffering and death not just relating to people 'over there' but now very much part of our lives.

Guli's reflections powerfully reveal that having the experience of disruption, trauma, suspicion and violence that most people in the world – especially the two-thirds world – know shows that life and death are very close and ever present. I am reminded that in John's Gospel water and blood flow from the side of Jesus (John 19.34) – that happens in death but of course also happens in birth. Death and birth are linked, which is also seen in baptism. Traditionally we see the waters as the waters of death and the emergence from them symbolic of the entry into new hope-filled life. Hidden in plain sight, our faith has invited us to live daily with the poles of life and death.

Like a musician who relies on body memory in their fingers playing their instruments, so I notice, first, a kind of body memory in Guli's reflections about the cross of Jesus. However, it is not just her memories of sudden trauma, of tentative belonging, of the quest for community and of the 'fear [of] the terror of the night, or the arrow that flies by day' (Psalm 91.5). We see that the memories of Jesus' death as told in the Gospels are interwoven with her story to the point where the body memory of both stories is blurred so as to create another body memory – a Christian body memory.

I put it that way because it is neither rational nor sub-conscious nor emotional, but it is all these things held together in a life, in a body. It is human. Just as disruptive experience within trauma leaves a body memory with the survivor, so there is something in the words of Jesus from the cross shaping another life that is disconcerting and yet fulfilling. This is embodied Christianity. After such an experience of suffering and death, the tomb or the quietude of a graveyard gives the necessary space and atmosphere for creating contemplation. This is not born of slick prayer practices or spiritual tricks but rather a contemplation connected with being with, being present to, recognising what is being done to us as much as any response that might come from us. This is about presence and our gaze and attention.

Second, I notice that because Holy Saturday has a full rather than an empty tomb, our reflections are taken towards presence rather than absence. There is a body and it is dead. Coming from Northern Ireland, I am still familiar with spending time with bodies that have died, as often they are brought home before a funeral on the third day. As a young teenager I remember being found alone in the bedroom with my granny in her coffin, chatting away aware of her dead presence. I took similar time with my sister's body in her coffin. Both were very different circumstances of death yet both were marked by common human stories. However, it is the particularity of each that resonates in my memory, and so too with Guli's reflections.

When we hear the same Bible reading being read in a variety of languages, we recognise that it is both the same story and yet a multiplicity of stories. Even a different accent makes us conscious of the diversity. Suddenly here the power of the cross has a setting and place amid the extraordinary tiles and architecture and fountains of Isfahan. Imagining a group of Iranian neighbours embracing after news of a killing in the Islamic Revolution reframes the emergence of a Christian community beyond narrow familial ties, as we know of John and Mary. Our visions of heaven now can include the shady arbours and fountains of an Islamic or Iranian garden. The experience of carrying our impostor syndromes or our experiences of rejection and being outsiders get connected into those of refugees and asylum seekers as well as the 'rejected ... man of sorrows, and acquainted with grief' (Isaiah 53.3, KJV).

Our mental illness, our depression and despair find familiarity in the forsakenness of others and in the silence that affords them space and dignity to be what they are without making them into our experience or trying to sort them out.

Serene Jones, who is President of Union Theological Seminary in New York, has written about this kind of God-talk in her book *Call it Grace*.[15] It is a narrative of life and faith, of Scripture and tradition, of church and world. It has many echoes with Guli's approach. Serene makes a distinction between theology and religion, making it clear that her concerns are theological not religious. She notes that religions focus on order, codified belief and much concern about the boundaries. However, theology rises above all that to ask the bigger questions about meaning not held by experts but rather understood as a universal human endeavour. I agree with her that we have too much religion, including lots of bad religion, and not enough theology. There is a challenge here for anyone in Christian leadership let alone a bishop: How much theological insight can be offered as opposed to the insatiable demands for religious leadership?

People sometimes comment that in a crisis the Church is too silent; too self-aware and driven by its own communications strategies. Leaders know that it is not always easy to be heard and certainly not always possible to communicate straightforwardly, owing to the riven differences within the Christian community, never mind the narrower field of the Church of England. However, there is also a pull or force towards concentrating more on the Church and its religion and much less on the wider world, especially as the religious institutions struggle with not enough numbers, not enough money, and their attendant anxiety.

Holy Saturday thoughts take us back to the mystery of life and death and to what can be said about these things alongside what cannot be said about them. Deep personal reflection on the death of Jesus has in every generation opened up the theological space. The 'being with this story' opens it up not only in the Church but in the world, as in every generation it is taken up again by our artists, musicians and writers. Reducing this to a religious story removes it from the world – the world God in Jesus came to save. It also can remove it from the Church when it becomes a religious story, because the Church mistakes it for religion rather than theology and is thus unaware of speech that might belong to God.

Holy Saturday invites us to stay with the story that has led to the death of Jesus, understood in the lives of ordinary people and made vivid by those from a persecuted or minority background. It is as if the paradoxes of life and death, dark and light, thirst and quenching and every other one can only be really held together if we refuse to avoid the tomb that speaks of our death, our pains and our losses. According to St Luke, the dead body of Jesus was placed into the tomb by a group of friends. It was given care, wrapped in a cloth. The women prepared the spices and ointments. So even in the profound aloneness of the cross and death, the new community is already emerging long before there is any sign of resurrection. We see that care and hope are not simply gifts of Easter but rather are gifts to be seen in every aspect of life, even in the experience of suffering and death.

Guli quotes her father at the height of the Iranian Revolution – 'we are learning the meaning of faith in a new and deeper way'. I now see I was wrong to start with the questions 'What is there to be said?' or 'What is there to be done?' Instead Guli's journey with Jesus reminds me that these unsurprising human questions are maybe not the best ones because they try to solve things too quickly, try to put me back in control and to seek answers that are not available to us. Instead, the task is both in silence and speech, in being and doing to bring our whole selves with our very particular stories to the very particular story of Jesus, and through grace and by the power of the Spirit be formed into his likeness. This will reshape our sense of self and belonging and mould us with body memory into a new human community.

The Letter to Peter sums it up well:

> Come to him, a living stone, though rejected by mortals yet chosen and precious in God's sight, and like living stones, let yourselves be built into a spiritual house ... Once you were not a people, but now you are God's people; once you had not received mercy, but now you have received mercy. (1 Peter 2.4–5a, 10)

That letter is written to isolated and persecuted Christians following the way of Christ. Now at a very different time and in a very different place, we hear the witness of a Christian with similar experience returning us to our hope and our identity. Through the Scriptures, our speech and silence, the days of Good Friday, Holy Saturday and ultimately Easter Day are freed to be properly theological – the deepest words possible about us and about God. Who knows: that might lead to more speech or indeed to different actions, but only if we discover in Guli's own words that 'Faith is at once both a journey into exile and a joyful homecoming.'

The Very Revd David Monteith
Dean of Leicester and Chair of the Church of England
College of Deans

Out
Of a great need
We are all holding hands
And climbing.
Not loving is a letting go.
Listen,
The terrain around here
Is
Far too
Dangerous
For
That.

Hafiz, version by David Ladinsky[16]

Notes

1 Hafiz, 'The Diamond Takes Shape', in *The Gift: Poems by Hafiz, the Great Sufi Master*. London: Penguin, 1999. Used by permission of the translator Daniel Ladinsky.

2 John Connolly, *The Book of Lost Things*. London: Hodder & Stoughton, 2006, dedication page.

3 Guli Francis-Dehqani, *Religious Feminism in an Age of Empire: CMS Women Missionaries in Iran, 1869–1934*. Bristol: CCSRG, University of Bristol, 2000.

4 Lavinia Greenlaw, 'The Refusal of Place', in *The Essay: Odes to Essex*. Broadcast on BBC Radio 3 on 3 January 2021.

5 Farifteh Robb, *In the Shadow of the Shahs: Finding Unexpected Grace*. Oxford: Lion Hudson, 2020, p. 11.

6 To learn more about the history of the Anglican Church in Iran and the impact of the Islamic Revolution, see e.g. Gordon Hewitt, *The Problems of Success: A History of the Church Missionary Society 1910–1942, Volume 1*. London: SCM Press, 1971, pp. 375–402; H. B. Dehqani-Tafti, *The Hard Awakening*. London: Triangle, 1981; H. B. Dehqani-Tafti (ed. Kenneth Cragg), *The Unfolding Design of my World: A Pilgrim in Exile*. Norwich: Canterbury Press, 2000.

7 Annette Simmons, *The Story Factor: Inspiration, Influence, and Persuasion through the Art of Storytelling*. New York: Basic Books, 2006, p. xix.

8 Ibid., p. xx.

9 This English translation of the prayer can be found in George Appleton (ed.), *The Oxford Book of Prayer*. Oxford: Oxford University Press, 1985, p. 135. I have modified the language to make it more accessible.

10 Cited in Bill Shipsey, 'Václav Havel Ambassador of Conscience 2003: From Prisoner to President – A Tribute', *Archive*.

today, 2003, http://web.archive.org/web/20060621133537/http://www.artforamnesty.org/aoc/biog_havel.html (accessed 19.2.21).

11 Anne Tyler, *Digging to America*. London: Vintage, 2007.

12 Henri Nouwen, *In the Name of Jesus: Reflections on Christian Leadership*. London: Darton, Longman & Todd, 1989.

13 The Church Missionary Society (now the Church Mission Society) produced a poster with these words printed on it (1980).

14 Martin Laird, *Into the Silent Land: The Practice of Contemplation*. London: Darton, Longman & Todd, 2006, p. 132.

15 Serene Jones, *Call it Grace: Finding Meaning in a Fractured World*. New York: Viking, 2019.

16 Hafiz, 'A Great Need', in *The Gift*. Used by permission of Daniel Ladinsky.